THE SACRISTAN
in the Catholic Church

A PRACTICAL GUIDE

TIMOTHY V McDONALD

First published in 1999 by
KEVIN MAYHEW LTD
Buxhall
Stowmarket
Suffolk IP14 3BW

© 1999 Timothy V McDonald

ISBN 1 84003 440 8
Catalogue No. 1500306

Cover design by Jaquetta Sergeant
Illustrated by Graham Johnstone
Typesetting by Louise Selfe
Printed in Great Britain

CONTENTS

THE AUTHOR

Timothy McDonald is Master of Ceremonies and Sacristan at the National Shrine of Our Lady at Walsingham, Norfolk. Prior to this he lived in London, where he was an altar server at Westminster Cathedral for about 18 years. His childhood parish was in the Diocese of Southwark, where he had served Mass from the age of six, and was Sacristan and Master of Ceremonies for many years.

He was appointed co-ordinator for the recent centenary celebrations of the National Shrine and has had two books published, *One Hundred Years of Pilgrimage, 1897-1997* and *A Year of Celebration*, both of which are compilations relating to the centenary of modern-day pilgrimage to Walsingham, celebrated between August 1997 and September 1998.

FOREWORD

While I have been writing the final chapters of this book, the national and religious newspapers, the television and radio news have all been full of the news of the death, funeral and burial of Cardinal George Basil Hume OSB.

As stated in my biography opposite, I served Mass at Westminster Cathedral for nearly twenty years, most of them during Cardinal Hume's archiepiscopate. My memories of him are too many to be noted here, but I would like to dedicate this small volume to his memory.

One of the many obituaries of the Cardinal that I have read quoted him as saying, 'It does not matter, to my mind at any rate, whether we sing in Latin or the vernacular, but it does matter that our worship be done with dignity and reverence.'

The sacristan who remembers that quotation will not go far wrong. I hope that this book will help to foster an attitude of dignity and reverence as well as furthering the sacristan's knowledge of what is correct and why it is so.

I would like to thank the following for their assistance in the preparation of this book: The Rev. Alan Williams sm and the Rev. Martin Fears for their valuable suggestions and advice. Anne Milton and Debbie Parker for proof reading the manuscript. Trevor Copperwheat for being my 'guinea-pig' in preparing certain liturgies from the manuscript. Finally, I owe a large thank you to Sister Rose Revilles sm, Paul Cook and Tom Coleman, my fellow sacristans at the National Shrine of Our Lady, for it is they who work with me to the standards outlined in these pages.

TVM

A PRAYER

Our Father,
may everything that I do
begin with your inspiration,
continue with your help,
and reach perfection under your guidance.

With your loving care guide my daily actions
and help me to persevere
with love and sincerity.

May the work I do bring growth in this life
to me and those I serve.

I unite my work
with the sacrifice of Jesus in the Mass
that it may be pleasing to you
and give you glory.

I beg your blessing upon all my efforts.

Help me to do the work you have asked
and come to the reward
you have promised.

Amen

Chapter 1

WHAT IS A SACRISTAN?

The *Pocket Oxford Dictionary* has the following entry:

Sacrist, sacristan, nn., official keeping
sacred vessels and vestments of a church.

That is the essence of the job, but a more complete definition is required for our purposes. The following job description is to be found in the *Ceremonial of Bishops*, revised by decree of the Second Vatican Ecumenical Council, and published by the Authority of Pope John Paul II in a translation printed by The Liturgical Press, Collegeville, Minnesota in 1989.

Sacristan

> 37. Along with the master of ceremonies and under his direction, the sacristan sees to the preparation for a celebration with a Bishop. The sacristan should carefully arrange the books needed for the proclamation of the word, and for the presidential prayers; he or she should lay out the vestments and have ready whatever else is needed for the celebration. He or she should see to the ringing of the bells for celebrations. He or she should ensure the observance of silence and quiet in the sacristy and the vesting room. Vestments, church furnishings and decorative objects that have been handed down from the past are not to be treated carelessly, but kept in good condition. When anything new needs to be provided, it should be chosen to meet the standards of contemporary art, but not out of a desire simply for novelty.

> 38. The first of all elements belonging to the beauty of the places where the liturgy is celebrated is the spotless

cleanliness of the floor and walls and of all the images and articles that will be used or seen during a service. In all the liturgical appurtenances both ostentation and shabbiness are to be avoided; instead the norms of noble simplicity, refinement, gracefulness, and artistic excellence are to be respected. The culture of the people and local tradition should guide the choice of objects and their arrangement, 'on condition that they serve the places of sacred worship and the sacred rites with the reverence and honour due to them'.

The adornment and decor of a church should be such as to make the church a visible sign of love and reverence toward God, and to remind the people of God of the real meaning of the feasts celebrated there and to inspire in them a sense of joy and devotion.

That is how the Church describes the sacristan in an official Vatican Council document, but some flesh can be usefully added to the council's words.

Father Dennis Murphy, in his *Sacristan's Manual* (Burns Oates 1950), has the following to say and it is still relevant today, even though fifty years have passed and a Vatican Ecumenical Council has taken place.

A sacristan must be chosen who is reliable and will carry out the responsible duties faithfully and meticulously. His (her) principal duties are to see that the sacred vestments, vessels, books, candles, ornaments and instruments for use in the church and on the altar, and other ecclesiastical furniture, be kept whole, entire and clean and he (she) should see that what is worn out should be renewed and what is torn should be mended.

He (she) must see that the sanctuary is kept spotlessly clean and tidy, that the sanctuary lamp burns continuously, that holy water is frequently renewed and stoops filled, and indeed see that the church is kept worthy of its purpose.

He (she) is responsible for the decoration of the church and altars on feast days for Mass and other ceremonies and special mention is made of the High Altar, credence, tribunes, choir and sacristy, and that everything is prepared and put in its correct place before each ceremony. He (she) is made responsible for the ringing of the church bell to indicate the time of Mass . . .

He (she) must see that quietness and order are maintained in the sacristy and he (she) is thus responsible for the conduct of the altar servers and other layfolk who have to use the sacristy for their legitimate business.

The sacristan's duties are by no means limited to the preparation for ceremonies, and indeed a great part of his (her) time is taken up with the care and maintenance of the sacristy itself. Strictly speaking his (her) field of action is restricted to the sanctuary and sacristy, and the cleaning of the church is more than he (she) can undertake; but in practice he (she) is a caretaker and although he (she) cannot be expected to carry out the entire work of keeping the church clean, he (she) will usually be responsible for those who do this.

The Sacristy Manual, one of the Archdiocese of Chicago's Liturgy training manuals published in 1993, describes the sacristan's job as involving the following elements:

1 Supervision of the Calendar
2 Prepare specific seasons and liturgies
3 Establish standard operating procedures
4 Maintain the church complex
5 Prepare liturgical materials
6 Maintain images and decorations
7 Take inventory
8 Minister at major liturgies
9 Perform other administrative duties

Notice that all three quotations have the same elements in common, even though the language and the dates may be very different. They give the sacristan's responsibilities as these:

- the liturgical books
- the sacred vestments
- the altar and its linen
- the sacred vessels
- cleanliness of the sanctuary, sacristy and church
- candles and lamps
- order and quiet in the sacristy
- the ringing of bells
- the keeping of rotas
- the ordering of supplies

The following chapters will deal with these topics, but first we need to consider the sacristy itself.

Chapter 2

THE SACRISTY

To quote once again from the *Ceremonial of Bishops*:

> 53. The (cathedral) church should have a vesting room,
> that is, a suitable place, as close as possible to the church
> entrance, where the bishop, concelebrants, and ministers
> can put on their liturgical vestments and from which the
> entrance procession can begin.
>
> The Sacristy, which should normally be separate from
> the vesting room, is a room where vestments and other
> liturgical materials are kept. It may also serve as the
> place where the celebrant and the ministers prepare for
> a celebration on ordinary occasions.

The sacristan who is able to plan the sacristy for a new
church is fortunate indeed; most of us inherit a poorly
planned room or series of rooms to which little thought
has been given, rather than a purpose-built, and efficient
place in which to work – all too often the sacristy is
everyone's dumping ground, a situation to be avoided,
if at all possible.

Ideally the sacristy has three rooms, one for the vesting of
the clergy, one for the vesting of servers and preparing
items for use in a liturgy, and finally, one where the dirty
work is done. Where this is not possible, and there is
only one room, it is essential that each area is clearly
defined, so that the messier items, such as charcoal and
flowers, are kept clear of the vestments and vessels.

Going back to the ideal, in the first room, the clergy vesting
room, are stored the various vestments, either in deep
wardrobes or in vestment chests. There must be at least
one surface where vestments can be laid out, more in a

large church, where concelebrants and deacons also vest. All too often vestments are not stored correctly; not only does this shorten their life, but it is also the cause of liturgies looking shabby and poorly prepared. A full-length mirror is essential.

The second room should have storage for the liturgical books, altar linen, frontals, hanging space for servers' robes (and choir robes if they have nowhere else to dress). There should be a table or desk and at least one chair. This table or another surface is where the requisites for Mass will be laid out before their transfer to the church and sanctuary.

The third room should be provided with at least one sink, although a second is very useful. Candles and items for occasional use are stored here, together with all cleaning items for the church and sacristan's use. One area should be fireproofed and used for the thurible, charcoal and incense. A safe large enough to store the sacred vessels is essential, and preferably a second safe, for keys and items of secular use or monies which are kept in the sacristy. The code of canon law requires that the tabernacle key should be kept securely when not in use. The registers should be kept in a secure and fire-proof cabinet or safe.

If there is nowhere else for flower arranging, it should happen here and separate storage should be available for vases, oasis and the other floristry items.

In a newly built church, the guidelines quoted from the *Ceremonial of Bishops* should be acted upon. The vesting room would then be near the entrance of the church to facilitate processions and can be used for the vesting of everyone – priests, deacons, choir, and servers. The second sacristy needs to be close to the worship area, so that materials to be laid out prior to a liturgy can be prepared and put out easily. It would still be preferable if this room were in two sections, one 'clean' and one 'dirty', as detailed above.

Each sacristy should have a crucifix prominently displayed and, in the area from which processions begin, there should be a bell or a light to alert the organist and a holy water stoop for the use of those in the procession. The name of the bishop should be prominently displayed, along with the name of any local saint to be included in the eucharistic prayer. The Diocesan Ordo (Calendar) and Year Book are useful here, as is a Service Record Book, notepad and pens. Copies of the *Eucharistic Prayers arranged for Concelebrations* should be available in the vesting room to be handed to concelebrants along with any service sheet or hymn book.

In a large complex, both the vesting room and sacristy should have telephone extensions, but with provision to silence them during services.

Within the sanctuary or sacristy a *piscina* or *sacrarium* (a sink whose outlet flows into the ground), should be sited where water used to wash the celebrants' hands after communion, or to purify the sacred vessels, can be poured. It is inappropriate to dispose of this water down a normal sink!

If the sacristy or vesting room is used for the children's Liturgy of the Word, there should be a table, two candles and a missal stand left available.

The Sacristy Furniture

The Vestment Press with Cupboard

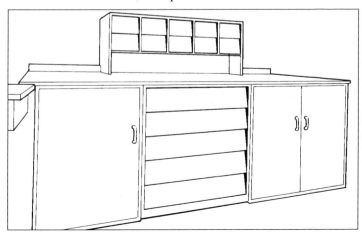

Chapter 3

THE LITURGICAL BOOKS

The efficient sacristan has an intimate working knowledge of the books used in the various liturgies. He or she should know what each volume contains, and know their way around it. They should be able to assist the priest with the choice of complementary texts from within the Missal and the Lectionary.

Foremost amongst the books are *The Roman Missal, The Lectionary, The Rites* and *The Book of the Gospels.*

At the front of each book is found the relevant Vatican Council document, which includes information of great importance and interest to the sacristan in his or her preparations for the various liturgies. These documents should be read very carefully, in particular *The General Instruction of the Roman Missal* (GIRM) to be found at the front of the Missal.

Listed below are the principal books and their contents:

THE ROMAN MISSAL

> *Decrees of the Sacred Congregation for Divine Worship*
> *Apostolic Constitution of Pope Paul VI*
> *General Instruction on the Roman Missal (GIRM)*
> *General Norms for the Liturgical Year and Calendar*
> *General Roman Calendar*
> *Table of Movable Feasts*
> The Proper of the Seasons
> Solemnities of the Lord in Ordinary Time
> Solemn Blessings
> Order of Mass with a congregation
> Order of Mass: musical setting

Order of Mass without a congregation
Proper of the Saints
Common Masses
Ritual Masses
Masses and Prayers for various occasions
Votive Masses
Masses for the Dead
National Calendars
National Propers

Appendices
   I   *Missale Romanum (Missale Parvum)*
   II   *Rite of blessing and sprinkling water*
   III *Sample formulae for general intercessions*
   IV *Musical setting of the order of Mass*
   V   *Preparation for Mass*
   VI *Thanksgiving after Mass*

Indexes
   Alphabetical Index of Celebrations
   Index of Prefaces
   General Index

There are certain feasts which are always difficult to locate: The Most Holy Trinity, The Sacred Heart and Corpus Christi are to be found under the heading, 'Solemnities of the Lord in Ordinary Time', and the Immaculate Heart of Mary is to be found at the end of May in the Proper of Saints.

The Roman Missal is available in a smaller (A6) facsimile edition as *The Saint Luke's Daily Missal* and is a very useful book for daily use at the Chair, or at liturgy planning meetings.

On Sundays and certain Feasts, a book called a *Sacramentary* is available to be used at the Chair. (There is some confusion over the term 'sacramentary', as this

THE LITURGICAL BOOKS 17

should correctly be used for *The Roman Missal*. A Missal traditionally has the readings in it, which *The Roman Missal* does not. Perhaps the Liturgical Commission for England and Wales will correct this when the new *Roman Missal* is published.)

There are separate books available with the complete *Services of Holy Week* in them. It is useful to have three copies, especially if it is usual for the Passion to be recited in its parts.

The second of the liturgical books is *The Lectionary*. This is set out in three volumes, and is available in two sizes, a larger version for use at the lectern, and a smaller set (A5) that is useful for less formal celebrations, study, discussion or prayer groups and liturgy planning meetings.

THE LECTIONARY

Volume One:

The Proper of Seasons
   The Season of Advent
   The Season of Christmas
   The Season of Lent
   The Easter Triduum
   The Season of Easter
   Feasts of the Lord in Ordinary Time
     (Most Holy Trinity, Sacred Heart, Corpus Christi)
   Sundays of the Year in Ordinary Time Year A
   Sundays of the Year in Ordinary Time Year B
   Sundays of the Year in Ordinary Time Year C
   Holy Days, Feasts of the Lord and Solemnities
   National Calendars

Index with biblical references

Volume Two:

Weekdays in Ordinary Time
Proper of Saints
Commons

Weekdays in Ordinary Time Year I
Weekdays in Ordinary Time Year II

Proper of Saints
   General Roman Calendar
   National Calendars

The Commons
   Common of Dedication of a Church
   Common of the Blessed Virgin Mary
   Common of Martyrs
   Common of Pastors
   Common of Doctors
   Common of Virgins
   Common of Holy Men and Women

Index with biblical references

(Once again, the Immaculate Heart of Mary is to be found
at the end of May, as in *The Roman Missal*.)

Volume Three:

Ritual Celebrations
Masses for Various Needs/Occasions
Votive Masses
Masses for the Dead

Ritual Celebrations
   Christian Initiation
   Eucharist
   Penance

Rites of the Sick and the Dying
Marriage
Holy Orders
Ministries
Blessing of Persons
Rites of Dedication of Church and Altar

Masses for Various Needs and Occasions
I   For The Church
II   For Civil Needs
III   For Various Public Needs
IV   For Particular Needs

Votive Masses

Masses for the Dead

Index with biblical references

The third of the essential books for use in the liturgies is:

THE RITES

Volume One:

Christian Initiation
    Rite of Christian Initiation of Adults
    Rite of Baptism for Children
    Rite of Confirmation
Rite of Penance
Holy Communion and Worship of the Eucharist outside
    Mass
Rite of Blessing of Oils
Rite of Consecrating Chrism
Rite of Marriage
Pastoral Care of the Sick:
    Rites of Anointing and Viaticum
Order of Christian Funerals

Volume Two:

Institution of Readers and Acolytes
Ordination of Deacons, Priests and Bishops
Rite of Religious Profession
Blessing of Persons: Abbot, Abbess
Consecrating to a Life of Virginity
Rite of Commissioning Special Ministers of Holy
    Communion
Dedication of a Church and Altar

The first volume of *The Rites* obviously has more relevance
in a parish than the second, and each of the sections is
now available separately in book form, which is more
convenient for use in a liturgical setting. These separate
volumes are usually kept by the priest for his use in
ascertaining the form a marriage, baptism or funeral, for
example, is going to take. The full volume is useful for the
sacristan preparing for a celebration because, by reading
through the rubrics contained in the various sections, he
or she can find what needs to be prepared prior to the
ceremony or liturgy. Close liaison is vital between the celebrant and the sacristan, so that the latter knows what form,
prayers and readings are to be used for a particular rite.

These, then, are the three major liturgical books essential
in every sacristy for the celebration of ceremonies of the
Roman Rite. In practice, however, other books may be
needed and it is suggested that some or all of the following
should be available on the sacristy bookshelves.

There are available some magnificently produced *Books
of the Gospels* and it is desirable that one be carried by the
deacon in the entrance procession of a solemn Mass.
However, care must be taken that the version purchased
for use by a parish contains the permitted texts and not
their American counterpart. The use of photocopied or

computer generated sheets with the New Jerusalem Bible texts inserted into an ornamental cover is not really acceptable: it is supposed to be a *Book of the Gospels*, not a loose-leaf file!

Some think that, as the *Book of the Gospels* is a gift from the Bishop at the consecration of a church, this book can only be used in a consecrated building. The liturgists and rubricists are still fighting it out, but in practice a *Book of the Gospels* is in use in many parishes.

The *Sacramentary* is the book for use at the Chair on Sundays and certain feasts, containing the Opening and Communion Prayers from the Proper of the Mass, together with the penitential rites, solemn blessings and the rites of dismissal.

It is useful to have a book of *Prayers of the Faithful for Sundays*, and another with the *Prayer of the Faithful for Weekdays*. Many parishes choose to write their own bidding prayers, but this must only be done with full guidance from the celebrant. In many places this prayer is omitted on weekdays, but the GIRM states: 'It is appropriate that this prayer is included in all Masses celebrated with a congregation'. Sample forms for seasonal use can be found in Appendix III of *The Roman Missal*.

Several copies of the following three books should be available in the vesting room, especially if concelebrations are a regular part of the parish liturgy cycle.

1. *The Eucharistic Prayers Arranged for Concelebration*
2. *The Eucharistic Prayers for Masses for Various Occasions*
3. *The Eucharistic Prayers for Masses with Children and Masses of Reconciliation*

The hymn book favoured by the parish should appear on the sacristy shelf, preferably in a music edition.

A *People's Daily Missal* and a *Sunday Missal* should be available for the reader, to enable them to lead the Entrance and Communion Antiphons when these are not sung, or replaced by hymns. GIRM 26 states that 'the entrance song is sung alternately by choir and people, or by cantor and people; or it is sung entirely by the people or the choir alone . . . If there is no singing at the entrance, the antiphon in the missal is recited either by the people, by some of them, or by a reader, otherwise it is said by the priest after the greeting'.

Where exposition and benediction of the Blessed Sacrament are celebrated, the book *Holy Communion and Worship of the Eucharist outside Mass: Volume 1. Rites* and *Volume 2. Readings* must be available. These outline the new rites for exposition and benediction. All too often parishes are still using the pre-conciliar *Ritus Servandus* and do not appear to have realised that these new rites exist! The format of any other regular parish devotions should be available in the sacristy.

Congregational copies of the following should be available:

Baptismal Rite
Rite of Reception into Full Communion
Rite of Christian Marriage
Funeral Rite

Mass Cards for those under instruction or those unfamiliar with the Roman Liturgy are also very useful.

Two further books recommended for the sacristy are first, *The Ceremonial of Bishops* (1989) which lays down the norms for every service, not only those where a bishop is present, and second *The Ceremonies of the Modern Roman Rite: The Eucharist and the Liturgy of the Hours, a manual for Clergy and all involved in Liturgical Ministries*, a modern *Fortescue and O'Connell* (the pre-Vatican II sacristan's 'bible').

All liturgical books are usually provided with page ribbons. These need to be reset for each celebration and are used to mark:

In *The Missal*:

> The Liturgy of the Eucharist
> The Prayer over the Gifts
> The Preface (sung or said)
> The Eucharistic Prayer
> The Communion Rite
> The Communion Antiphon

In *The Sacramentary* or Book at the Chair:

> The Entrance Antiphon
> The Introductory Rites
> The Prayer of the Faithful
> The Prayer after Communion
> The Concluding Rite
> The Solemn Blessing (when required)

In *The Lectionary*:

> The First Reading and Responsorial Psalm
> The Second Reading
> The Gospel Acclamation and Gospel

On most days the readings are gathered together and only one ribbon is needed to indicate their position, but when Masses are being said for particular needs, the other ribbons may be required.

Before a celebration, *The Missal* needs to be set, checked by or explained to the celebrant, placed on its stand or cushion and placed on the credence table. *The Lectionary*, once set and checked, is placed on the lectern. If it is to be carried in procession, it needs to be in the vesting part of the sacristy for the reader or deacon to collect. If the

Book of the Gospels is carried, this also needs to be marked and in the vesting room. The book for use at the Chair is placed near the Chair for a daily celebration, and either on the credence table or carried in procession by the book-bearer for a solemn liturgy.

In parishes where there is a Children's Liturgy of the Word there should be various copies of the Bible or Lectionary available for the different age groups. It is usual for the priest to hand the children's Bible to the group leader after the opening sign of the cross and greeting of the Mass, and it should be available either on the credence table or in the vesting room if carried in procession.

The bookshelf is now full, and it is time to consider the sacred vestments.

Wooden Altar Book Rest

Chapter 4

THE SACRED VESTMENTS

The Sacred Vestments are deliberately so called, because it must be remembered that that is what they are – sacred for use in the sacred mysteries – and they should be treated as such, with great care and attention. The Sacred Vestments are these:

The Alb
A white linen, cotton or polyester, sleeved garment which reaches from the neck to the ankle – often with a hood, cowl or stand-up collar to mask the shirt or collar beneath.

> The vestment common to all ministers is the alb tied at the waist with a cincture, unless it is made to fit without a cincture . . . A surplice may replace the alb, except when a chasuble or dalmatic is worn, or when a stole is used alone instead of a chasuble or dalmatic with stole. (GIRM 298)

> Ministers below the order of deacon may wear the alb or other vestment that is lawfully approved in the respective region. (GIRM 301)

The Amice
A covering for the neck and shoulders (traditionally square with two long fixing tapes although there are modern versions available with velcro fixings), especially worn under an alb that has no cowl or collar.

> If the alb does not completely cover the ordinary clothing at the neck, an amice should be worn under it. (GIRM 298)

The Cincture or Girdle

A white tassel-ended cord worn around the waist of some albs, traditionally used to anchor the stole.

> Anyone who wears an alb should use a cincture and an amice unless other provision is made. (GIRM 81)

The Stole

A long and narrow scarf-like vestment, the mark of ordination, the stole is worn by a priest around his neck and falling equally each side to his knees, and by a deacon over his left shoulder and falling to his right side. The deacon's stole is either looped in place, or sewn together to enable it to hang correctly. Many modern deacon's stoles are shaped to help them to hang flat. The stole reflects the colour of the liturgy to be celebrated, or the season of the Church's year.

> The priest wears the stole around his neck and hanging down in front. The deacon wears it over his left shoulder, crossed and fastened at the right side. (GIRM 302)

The Chasuble

Over all the preceding vestments, the priest wears the chasuble when he is to celebrate the Mass.

> The chasuble worn over the stole is the proper vestment of the priest who celebrates Mass or other services connected with Mass unless otherwise indicated. (GIRM 299)

There are various forms of the chasuble, but the best is a full garment with little superfluous decoration. Now that forward-facing altars are once again the norm, the Church desires that the post-conciliar liturgy show 'a noble simplicity'.

> The noble simplicity which reflects authentic art should be a major factor in selecting furnishings. (GIRM 237)

This is best attained by the use of the full- or half-Gothic, or medieval-shape chasuble. The Roman, Latin, Spanish, Fiddleback, or Baroque chasuble with heavily decorated back and pinched waist is inappropriate for modern liturgies.

> The beauty of a vestment should derive from its material and form, rather than from its ornamentation. (GIRM 306)

The chasuble, like the stole, is of a colour appropriate to the feast or season. An unfortunate habit has developed whereby at a concelebration only the principal celebrant wears a chasuble. The GIRM clearly states in section 161 on concelebrations:

> In the sacristy or other suitable place, the concelebrants put on the *usual vestments* for Mass. For a *good reason*, as when there are more concelebrants than vestments, the concelebrants *may* omit the chasuble but wear the stole over the alb. The celebrant *always* wears the chasuble.

The Dalmatic
A sleeved tunic worn by deacons over the alb and stole when assisting at the Mass.

> The dalmatic worn over the alb and stole is the vestment proper to the deacon. (GIRM 300)

The dalmatic is, like the stole and chasuble, of the colour appropriate to the feast or season; however, white may be worn if dalmatics of the other liturgical colours are not available. Traditionally the dalmatic has vertical bands of decoration *(orphreys)* from the shoulder to the hem and sometimes two horizontal bands as well.

The chasuble and dalmatic should, if possible, be stored flat with any folds vertically in line with the fall of the vestment. This prevents unsightly horizontal creases

appearing. These vestments can be hung on specially purchased broad-shouldered hangers, but use of a narrow coat
hanger can seriously disfigure the line of the shoulders.

The Cope

An ankle-length cloak of rich fabric with orphreys rising
from the hem at the front to the back of the neck, where
there is generally a hood. The cope is worn over the
cassock and cotta (see page 29) by ministers at the
Liturgy of the Hours, benediction, the sacraments outside Mass and for public processions. The cope is worn
over an alb and stole when a ceremony leads into the
Mass, as does the Blessing of Palms and Solemn Entry
on Passion Sunday. Of the colour of the feast or season,
the cope is not only a priestly vestment, but may be worn
by deacons, and on occasions by non-ordained ministers
(for example, cantors at the Liturgy of the Hours) as the
rubrics direct.

> The priest wears a cope in processions and other services,
> as indicated by the rubrics of each rite. (GIRM 303)

The Humeral Veil

A wide scarf, usually about nine feet in length and two
feet wide, placed around the shoulders of the priest or
deacon as he carries the Blessed Sacrament or Relics in
procession and when giving the blessing during the
Benediction. Usually white or matching the cope worn at
the time, the humeral veil is a sign of non-verbal respect
for the item carried.

> The priest or deacon should wear a white cope and
> humeral veil to give the blessing at the end of adoration,
> when the exposition takes place with the monstrance; in
> the case of exposition in the ciborium, the humeral veil
> should be worn. (Holy Communion and the Eucharist
> outside Mass 92)

The American sacristan's manual quoted from earlier includes one more item under the heading 'Sacred Vestments', and that is:

The (Funeral) Pall
A large cloth usually of white fabric, although some dioceses still allow purple or black, 'The Final Vestment' is placed over the mortal remains of a person during the Funeral Mass. The pall should be unadorned and is used to recall the (white) baptismal robe (the first vestment) and to express the hope that the deceased is in the realms of glory. This pall differs from the pall used to protect the contents of the chalice (see Chapter 5). The Bishop's Conference now allows the Union Flag to be used as a pall for service personnel.

Other garments are used by ministers during the sacred liturgies, but are not usually termed 'vestments'. Principal among these are:

The Cassock
A full-length, sleeved garment, the traditional street garb for a priest in Catholic countries. Used to distinguish the ordained from the laity, a priest or deacon usually wears a black cassock. A variety of coloured buttons and piping can be added to indicate higher rank. Bishops traditionally wear a purple cassock, Cardinals red and the Pope and priests in the tropics, white.

The Cotta or Surplice
Both of white linen, cotton or polyester, the cotta has a square neck which reveals the cassock beneath. The hem reaches to the fingertips when the hands fall at the sides, and the sleeves end half way down the forearm. The surplice is a much longer garment, reaching to the calf, with wide wrist-length sleeves and a round neck. The body of

the surplice is normally gathered at the neck band, whereas the cotta is usually attached in flat pleats.

In many churches, altar servers wear the cassock and cotta, the cassock sometimes being blue or red to differentiate between servers and priests. Some parishes dress their servers in albs and cinctures. It is important that servers only wear their cassocks or albs when on duty in the sanctuary. Visitors to a church should be able to differentiate between priest and servers by their mode of dress.

LAYING OUT OF VESTMENTS

In preparing for a liturgy, the sacristan should check the year book and diocesan calendar to see what colour is appropriate to the day, and should take into account any local feasts, or specific instructions from the priest. The best or finer vestments should be reserved for solemnities and feasts, in order to add extra dignity to festal occasions.

The first vestment to be laid out is the chasuble and this is best laid flat, face down on the vesting surface; the back can be folded up, but continually doing this does cause a horizontal crease to appear across the back of the vestment. The stole is then arranged on the chasuble in the shape of an 'H', its ends being in line with the shoulder, with the neck forming the crosspiece. As he vests, the priest should be able to kiss the back of the neck of the stole before placing it around his own neck. Next the cincture is placed on the stole, folded double and laid in the shape of an 'S'. The alb is put on top of the other vestments, its neck in line with the neck of the chasuble, the arms folded in to the waist. The body of the alb should be concertinaed on top, so that its weight does not cause the pile of vestments to slide to the floor. On top of the alb is placed the unfolded amice with its tapes separated to help the priest as he puts it around his shoulders and neck. The priest's cassock, if worn under the alb, should be left on its hanger nearby.

The same procedure is followed for the deacon's vestments, except that the dalmatic is laid out first, once again avoiding unnecessary horizontal folds. The deacon's stole is placed diagonally on top of the dalmatic, laid double, with the stole's neck at the left shoulder and its hem on the right side; the cincture, alb, amice and cassock are placed as for a priest.

This form of laying out of the sacred vestments allows for the priest or deacon to put them on in the correct order; cassock, amice, alb, cincture, stole and chasuble or dalmatic.

If the celebrant wears a radio microphone, this should be left with the laid out vestments so that he can put it on as he vests. It is important to check any batteries before each service, to make sure that they are fully charged.

When a cope is worn, it is best left on its hanger nearby. The sacristan should be on hand to assist the deacon or priest as he puts it on. The stole should be laid on the vesting surface, with the cotta or cincture and alb laid on it as for Mass.

The dignity of the liturgy is enhanced if priests and attendant ministers are dressed in vestments which are of the same or complementary design. Where vestments clash, they can cause a visual distraction to the congregation during a liturgy.

Each Church should have at least one matching set of dalmatic, chasuble and priestly and diaconal stoles in each liturgical colour. Where costs allow, three chasubles and two dalmatics, each with the appropriate stole, is the preferred option. It is now common practice for priests to have a diocesan vestment and these can add dignity to deanery or other occasions where priests are likely to concelebrate. The wearing of an alb and stole only to concelebrate is not the option preferred by the Church and is only to be permitted where there is 'good reason' (see GIRM 161, quoted on page 27).

A vestment set should have with it a chalice veil. The veil is used to cover the prepared chalice when it is placed on the credence table before Mass, 'on the side table: the chalice, corporal, purificator, and if needed a pall . . . The chalice should be covered with a veil, which may always be white' (GIRM 79c).

Certain items will appear in the sacristy on the occasion of an Episcopal Visitation. They will be brought by the bishop or his secretary, and should be treated with the care due to all liturgical items. The crosier is the bishop's staff of office, the mitre is the liturgical headgear of a bishop and is worn over a zucchetto (skullcap) and the pectoral cross is worn over the chasuble. A Metropolitan will have a pallium which is a white woollen band decorated with black crosses with a black tab at front and back and is worn around the neck and shoulders over the chasuble. The servers deputed to attend the bishop will wear vimps which are scarves of silk worn over the shoulders with ribbons tied at the front. The server holds the mitre or crosier through the silk. White gloves can be used if vimps are not available. On any occasion it is useful for the cross bearer to wear white gloves if the cross is of precious metal or delicate in form.

While considering the sacred vestments, *The General Instruction of the Roman Missal* has some other sections which are relevant:

281. In the sacristy the vestments for the priest and ministers should be prepared according to the form of celebration:

a) for the priest: alb, stole and chasuble;

b) for the deacon: alb, stole and dalmatic; the latter may be omitted if necessary or if less solemnity is desired;

c) for other ministers: albs or other vestments lawfully approved.

297. In the Body of Christ not all members have the same function, and this diversity of ministries is shown externally in worship by the variety of vestments. At the same time the vestments should contribute to the appearance of the rite itself.

304. The Conference of Bishops may determine adaptations in the forms of vestments which correspond to the needs and usages of their regions and propose these to the Apostolic See.

305. In addition to traditional materials, vestments may be made from natural fabrics of the region or manufactured fabrics in keeping with the dignity of the sacred action and the person wearing them. The Conference of Bishops will be the judges in this matter.

306. The beauty of the vestment should derive from its material and form rather than from its ornamentation. Ornamentation should include symbols, images or pictures suitable for liturgical use, and anything unbecoming should be avoided.

307. Colours in a vestment give an effective expression to the celebration of the mysteries of the faith and, in the course of the year, a sense of progress in the Christian life.

308. The traditional colours should be retained, namely:

a) White is used in the offices and Masses of the Easter and Christmas Seasons; on feasts and commemorations of the Lord, other than of his passion; on feasts and memorials of Mary, the angels, saints who were not martyrs, All Saints (1 November), John the

Baptist (24 June), John the Evangelist (27 December), the Chair of Peter (22 February), and the Conversion of Paul (25 January). White (silver) may be used in Masses for the dead*.

b) Red is used on Passion Sunday (Palm Sunday) and Good Friday, Pentecost, celebrations of the passion, birthday feasts of the apostles and evangelists, and feasts of martyrs.

c) Green is used in the offices and Masses of Ordinary Time.

d) Violet is used in Lent and Advent. It may also be used in offices and Masses for the Dead*.

e) Black may be used in Masses for the Dead and on All Souls Day (2 November)*.

f) Rose may be used on Gaudete Sunday (the Third Sunday of Advent) and Laetare Sunday (the Fourth Sunday of Lent).

The Conference of Bishops may determine adaptations suited to the needs and customs of the people and propose these to the Apostolic See.

309. On special occasions more noble vestments may be used, even if not the colour of the day.

310. Votive Masses are celebrated in the colour suited to the Mass itself, or in the colour of the day or season. Masses for various occasions are celebrated in the colour of the day or season*.

*Masses for the Dead are now celebrated in white (silver) or purple vestments rather than the black quoted above. The Church is waiting for a new edition of *The Roman Missal*, where the *General Instruction* may possibly be updated to reflect current thinking.

Chapter 5

THE ALTAR AND ITS LINEN

A section in the *General Instruction* concerns 'The arrangement and decoration of churches for the eucharistic celebration' and it is here that we find comments about the altar and we are told:

> The main altar should be free standing so that ministers can easily walk around it and Mass can be celebrated facing the people. It should be placed in a central position which draws the attention of the whole congregation. The main altar should be a fixed, consecrated altar. (GIRM 262).

Usually of stone, or other solid construction, the altar itself rarely needs much attention from the sacristan, but the opportunity given by the stripping of the altars on Holy Thursday should be taken to give the altar and its surface a good clean and polish.

Whilst discussing the altar a word must be said about the altar frontal (*antependium*). This is of the colour of the feast or the season and often matches the vestments in fabric and design. It is usually one of two types, either a laudian fall, which covers the altar on all four sides from the *mensa* (table) to the floor, or else it hangs from the front of the altar from a rail attached to the front face of the mensa. Great care must be taken in the design of the frontal; it must show the nature of the celebration, but not be so over-ornate as to distract from the liturgy being celebrated at the altar. Many churches have dispensed with the frontal and denote the season by the obligatory tabernacle veil and/or the optional lectern fall. All these hangings, the frontal, the lectern fall and the tabernacle veil, should be of a matching fabric, colour and design.

It is the tabernacle veil and lamp that indicate to the faithful that the Blessed Sacrament is reserved. In the Council Document *Holy Communion and Worship of the Eucharist outside Mass*, Section III says:

> The presence of the Eucharist in the tabernacle is to be shown by a veil or in another suitable way determined by the competent authority. According to traditional usage, an oil lamp or lamp with a wax candle is to burn constantly near the tabernacle as a sign of the honour which is shown to the Lord.

For the celebration of the Mass, the altar should be covered by at least one altar cloth. The older, pre-Vatican II practice of three cloths is no longer considered necessary. The altar cloth should be white and of a design suited to the style of the altar and church. A beautiful piece of ancient, embroidered linen, edged with lace, may be totally inappropriate in a modern church, whereas with a plain unadorned altar cloth one can seldom go wrong, whatever the setting. The altar cloth should cover the entire top of the altar and may hang down at the sides. During prolonged exposition and benediction a second or 'drip' cloth is used to protect the altar cloth from falling wax when extra-branched candlesticks are used. A dust cloth or cover should be placed over the altar when not in use.

Other items coming under the heading of altar linen are:

The corporal, a 16-18 inch square of fine starched linen adorned with one cross in its centre. The filled chalice(s), paten and the ciborium(a) with hosts are placed on the corporal at the offertory of the Mass and the celebrant makes it his intention to consecrate all the elements on the corporal. The corporal folded in three both on its length and breadth may be kept in a burse, which, like the chalice veil, is the colour of the liturgical season or feast. If used, the burse is placed on the top of the veiled chalice when the chalice is prepared for Mass.

The purificator, an oblong piece of white linen used to wipe the rim of the chalice between communicants at Holy Communion. Folded along its length in three, this is placed between the chalice and the paten when the chalice is prepared for the Mass. With the increased instances of distribution of Holy Communion under both species (kinds) a greater number of corporals are needed. The substitution of linen with paper napkins or fibrous products is not to be recommended. However, at very large celebrations involving communion under both species, if paper napkins are used they must be collected carefully and it would seem correct to burn them after the celebration.

The (chalice) pall, a square of stiffened linen, about six inches square, and used to cover the chalice to protect the contents from dust and flies. Placed over the paten with the celebrant's host, it helps the veil to hang well on the prepared chalice.

The prepared chalice is therefore 'layered' as follows: empty chalice, purificator (1), paten with celebrant's host (2), pall (3), chalice veil (4) and, on top, the burse containing the corporal. Where the burse is not used, the corporal should be placed on the pall under the veil. The chalice veil was traditionally sold with a vestment set, that is, chasuble, stole, chalice veil and burse together with a dalmatic and deacon's stole. Many modern sets do not have a chalice veil, and it has to be expressly ordered. Even more rare is the burse. The GIRM does however stipulate that a veil should be used.

> The chalice should be covered with a veil, which may always be white. (GIRM 80)

Preparing the Chalice

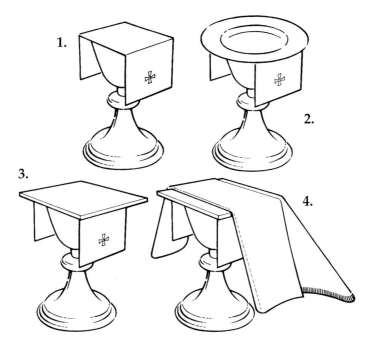

Other linens used regularly are the small white lavabo towel, for the drying of the priest's fingers during the Mass, and a credence cloth, often of similar design to the altar cloth, for the side table where the chalice and other items are placed prior to Mass.

Some items of linen are only used occasionally, such as other larger linen towels needed during the washing of the feet on Holy Thursday, and softer towels for the priest's hands on Ash Wednesday or whenever he has used the sacred oils.

The tabernacle and aumbry (the place where the holy oils are kept) should each be fitted with their own close-fitting corporal, which should be washed on the appropriate day in Holy Week, when these vessels are empty.

Any curtains inside the tabernacle should be cleaned at the same time.

All white altar linens should be immaculate as befits their use. Purificators and lavabo towels should only be used once, and they should be rinsed prior to washing. The rinsing water should be poured down the sacrarium. Ironing them whilst still damp will help to keep their shape. The corporal and pall should be washed regularly to stop them getting grubby. They should also be rinsed and the water thrown down the sacrarium. When these are ironed a small amount of starch is advisable, as this helps them maintain their creases and appearance; using a steam iron will make this job easier, and one should be available in the sacristy.

The Chalice

The Ciborium

The Paten

The Pyx

Chapter 6

THE SACRED VESSELS AND HOLY OILS

The sacred vessels are those used to contain the Sacred Body and Precious Blood of Christ during the Mass, or those used to reserve the sacrament in the tabernacle. They are called the chalice, the paten, the ciborium, the pyx and the lunette. The oil stocks are also considered in this grouping by virtue of the oils being consecrated at the Chrism Mass. Formularies for the blessing of the various vessels are to be found in *The Book of Blessings*.

The GIRM has the following sections about the sacred vessels:

289. Sacred vessels are necessary for the celebration of the Mass, and among these the chalice and the paten, because of the function they serve, are particularly important.

290. Vessels should be made from solid materials which are considered suitable in each region. The Conference of Bishops will be the judge in this matter. Materials which do not break or deteriorate easily are to be given preference.

291. Chalices and other vessels which are intended to hold the blood of the Lord should have a cup of non-absorbent material. The base may be of any other solid and worthy material.

292. Vessels which are intended to hold hosts, such as the paten, ciborium, pyx and monstrance, etc., may be made of other materials which are locally considered valuable and appropriate for sacred use such as ebony and hard woods.

293. It is suitable to use one large paten for the conse-cration of bread for the celebrant, ministers and faithful.

294. Vessels made from metal should ordinarily be gilded on the inside if the metal is one that oxidises; gilding is not necessary if the metal is one that does not oxidise.

295. The artist may give a form to the vessels which is in keeping with the culture of the area and their use in the liturgy.

296. The rites in the liturgical books should be used to bless or consecrate the sacred vessels.

Silver and gold set with precious stones or enamel are the traditional materials from which the sacred vessels are made in Europe and the West. It is essential that the vessels are kept perfectly clean, and this can be achieved with the various proprietary brands of metal polish and washing-up liquids. It is wise and recommended that once cleaned, the vessels are washed, rinsed and dried thoroughly to avoid any vestige of polish remaining, especially where there are heavily engraved surfaces and inscriptions. Jewels can be cleaned using a spirit such as alcohol (gin is particularly good, if it can be spared from the presbytery).

After use for communion each day it may not always be necessary to polish chalices, but washing in hot soapy water is recommended, as any trace of Precious Blood (wine) will eat into the gilding. It is good to have special towels in the sacristy solely to dry chalices and other vessels after washing. The general drying-up cloth is very often used inappropriately and should not be used on the sacred vessels.

The sacristan needs to be aware of the value of the sacred vessels. All too often there are unused chalices and monstrances, whose form has gone out of fashion, lying around in cupboards and presbyteries. These may not be fashionable, or need to be used, but they have been consecrated for a sacred purpose, and if they are of a good standard of workmanship it is likely that they are of value, especially to a thief or burglar. Sometimes the age of vessels is not appreciated – it has been known for a plain, dull-looking chalice to date from penal times*, and not be the worthless thing it appears to be. Most auction houses will date items and give a free valuation, and certainly items should be insured individually (when and where necessary), and not just collectively under the diocesan insurance.

The use of the chalice is obvious, but some of the other names used for the sacred vessels require a little explanation:

The paten is a circular disc, usually of gilded metal, on which the celebrant's host rests during the Mass.

The ciborium is either a lidded cup or open bowl, designed to hold the many hosts for the congregation at Mass. It is desirable that fresh hosts are consecrated at each Mass. The older custom of reserving larger numbers of the sacred hosts consecrated on Sundays for use during the week is no longer appropriate. The amount of the reserved sacrament should be sufficient to use for the sick, and to allow for some small margin of error in the daily consecration.

A pyx is a vessel designed to hold a small number of consecrated hosts for use when visiting the sick or housebound.

The term 'pyx' is also given to the metal case for the lunette, the holder for the host that is used for exposition and benediction. The lunette fits into the monstrance, a

*1563-1869, when Roman Catholicism was penalised in England.

showy vessel designed often as a starburst, or in the form of concentric rings often supported by angels or saints.

The stocks are small air-tight containers for the holy oils. The oils are those of Baptism, Chrism, and of the Sick (*Infirmarium*). The containers, usually silver, are marked 'B', 'C' and 'I' and are filled in the cathedral sacristy after the Chrism Mass on Holy Thursday. In some cases, the deanery stocks are filled then, and individual parishes approach their dean to have their stocks refilled. It is the sacristan's job to empty and clean the stocks before Holy Thursday, and to ensure that they are refilled for use at Easter. The unused oil can either be burnt with cotton wool or by using a wick, or added to the sanctuary lamp if it is an oil-burning one.

The stocks should be kept in a secure place, either in the church in an aumbry, or in the presbytery, so that the priest has swift access to them. Canon Law says:

1. In administering sacraments in which holy oils are to be used, the minister must use oil from olives or other plants, which . . . has recently been consecrated or blessed by a bishop. Older oil is not to be used except in a case of necessity.

2. The parish priest is to obtain the holy oils from his own bishop and keep them carefully in fitting custody. (Canon 847)

Most priests have their own single stock containing oil of the sick, which they keep on them, to enable sick calls to be made with the greatest haste.

Other vessels in the sacristy, though not strictly sacred vessels, are the cruets used to hold the water and wine. These can be of glass, pottery, precious or non-precious metal such as stainless steel. The lavabo bowl usually matches the cruets.

Care must be taken that fresh water and wine is always used for the celebration of the Mass. The sacristan who is responsible for ordering the wine and hosts must keep a stock adequate for the needs of the church; over-ordering leads to the hosts becoming stale or the wine becoming vinegar. Only natural alcoholic wine can be used for the Mass. The hosts for use at the Mass must be kept in an airtight container. With the increase in gluten-related allergies, gluten-free hosts are available, and should be kept for parishioners with this allergy. They are usually square, and can be placed on a separate paten or in a pyx to be consecrated to prevent them being mixed in with the hosts for the remainder of the congregation. Wafer boxes are available, holding about 100 host in groups of ten and can be useful during the week when there are smaller congregations. Flat silver tongs can be used by the people to place their host into the ciborium on arrival at Mass.

A decorated brass or silver vessel (*bucket*) and a brush or sprinkler (*aspergillium*) are needed on many occasions.

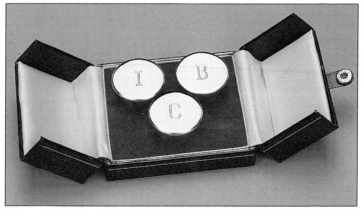

Three Single Holy Oil Stocks

Chapter 7

CLEANLINESS OF SANCTUARY, SACRISTY AND CHURCH

Most churches will have a roster of volunteer cleaners and it is the sacristan's job to keep this roster and to ensure that the cleaners are happy in their work. The cleanliness of the floors and carpets is the main concern, and vacuuming, polishing and dusting are very important if the church is to remain a fit setting for the sacred liturgies. Certain areas will need special attention prior to particular liturgies, for instance the font and baptistry area prior to a baptism.

Before the major feasts of the church, and prior to an Episcopal Visitation, a certain amount of spring cleaning may take place, but ideally the same standards should be maintained all year, for it is the House of God that is being cared for and its cleanliness should not depend on the Church's season or an impending visitation.

After each service, the sacristan should check around the church, and clear up anything such as hymn books or service sheets left behind.

Where a church serves as a resting place for the home-less, or those living on the streets, it is essential that any spillages of food, drink or any other matter are cleared away and the area cleaned properly, with disinfectant if necessary.

Chapter 8

CANDLES AND LAMPS

The GIRM has this general comment in code 269:

> Candles are required during liturgical services to express devotion or the degree of festivity. They should be placed either on the altar or around it, in harmony with the construction of the altar and sanctuary. The candles should not block the view of what is happening at the altar or what is placed on it.

For a daily Mass, two candles are the norm, whereas on a Sunday or Feast day, four or six candles can be used. A seventh candle is optional when a bishop presides at a liturgy.

> Mass with a congregation . . . on or near [the altar] are placed a cross and at least two lighted candles. Four or six candles may be used or, if the diocesan bishop celebrates, seven. The cross and candles may be carried in the entrance procession. (GIRM 79)

The document on *Worship of the Eucharist outside Mass* states that 'for exposition of the Blessed Sacrament in the monstrance, four to six candles are lit as at Mass . . . for exposition in the ciborium at least two candles should be lit'(II.85). Candles at shrines and by images around the church should be extinguished during periods of exposition and the service of benediction. The custom of visiting a statue of Our Lady for the seasonal anthem after benediction is to be recommended and a taper should be available to re-light any candles there.

During the Easter season, the paschal candle should be lit during liturgies, but not during benediction.

The custom of burning extra candles during a prolonged period of exposition is traditional, and can foster in the congregation a renewed respect for the Eucharist, a respect that seems to have diminished since the liturgical reforms of the Second Vatican Council. The five- or seven-branched candlesticks traditionally used for this should be kept clean, even if only occasionally used.

Candles are used on various feasts of the Church, for example on 2 February, when Candlemas is celebrated, and candles should be blessed before the principal Mass and carried in procession to recall the Presentation of Christ in the Temple. Two of the candles blessed on Candlemas are used the following day to bless throats on the feast of St Blaise. It is usual to carry candles in processions of the Blessed Sacrament and in processions during All-Night Vigils. All processional candles should be provided with a shade or guard to prevent wax being spilt in the church or over the person carrying the candle, and to help keep the candle alight while it is being carried.

The sacristan is responsible for the ordering of candles, preferably from an ecclesiastical supplier, where the quality and wax content is in accordance with church use. Domestic and coloured candles have no place in the liturgy, but may be used where there is a meditation chapel or icon displayed for contemplative prayer.

The ordering and preparation of the paschal candle is a major event in the working life of the sacristan. It is not obligatory to use the transfer provided – a free-hand painted emblem embellished with flowers can be very effective. When considering the purchase of the paschal candle, the size and design of the stand must be borne in mind. The metal studs containing incense grains must be emptied, cleaned and renewed when the candle is being prepared for use in the Easter Vigil. If the candle is to be carried outside, a glass shade should be used to protect the flame.

At Pentecost, the paschal candle is placed in the baptistry or near to the font.

> After the Easter season, the Easter candle should be given a place of honour in the baptistry, so that when it is lighted for the celebration of baptism, the candles of the newly baptised may be easily lighted from it. (Document on Christian Initiation 25)

Votive lights are also ordered by the sacristan and the stand for them needs daily attention.

Wax can be very destructive and disfiguring on altar cloths, vestments and carpets. The tried and tested way of removing it is to use a warm iron and brown paper. The paper is placed over the stain and the warm iron melts the wax which is then absorbed by the brown paper. It is essential to remove wax before items are washed, as after washing an impregnated mark remains which is impossible to remove. Wax on metal work, brass or silver candlesticks can be removed with boiling water without harming the metal, which should then be cleaned with a proprietary metal cleaner. Wax on wooden floors can be removed carefully with a wallpaper scraper.

While discussing candles, the snuffer, a conical metal device used to extinguish candles without spilling any molten wax, should also be considered. The cleaning of this is often forgotten, but the build-up of wax and smoke must be removed regularly as it leaves a black stain if spilt on linen. This stain is only removable with the strongest of modern cleaners which may permanently harm the fabric.

Candle caps *(followers)* can be placed over the tops of candles to help them to burn evenly. These are usually made of ceramic or other heat-proof material. Glass or card rings *(bobeches)* can be placed around the foot of a candle to stop molten wax from running over the candlestick.

Spring-loaded metal containers inside fake plastic candles were very popular in the 1960s and are sometimes used where very tall candles are needed to maintain the visual integrity of an altar. These are not ideal for daily use in the liturgy, as they are difficult to keep clean and not very reliable.

Oil- or gas-filled fake candles are not really acceptable for use in the liturgy. There is no provision in the documents of the church for the lamp burning at the tabernacle to be electric; it should be either oil or a candle:

> According to traditional usage, an oil lamp or a lamp with a wax candle is to burn constantly near the tabernacle as a sign of honour which is shown to the Lord. (Document on Holy Communion and the Eucharist outside Mass III, 2)

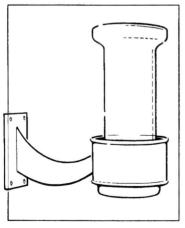

Two Types of Sanctuary Lamp

Chapter 9

ORDER AND QUIET IN THE SACRISTY

It is one of the tasks of the sacristan to maintain order in the sacristy, especially amongst the young servers prior to a liturgy. This needs to be done in an acceptable manner, with regard for the child protection laws and regulations.

The sacristan should never slap, cuff or touch a server, nor should he or she be alone in the sacristy with a child. Any training or rehearsal of servers should take place with another adult, preferably a parent or teacher, present.

If young servers are to respect the acts they are performing as part of the liturgy, this must be instilled into them by example and teaching. If they are given an understanding of the sacredness of what they are doing, if they are able to appreciate that the sacred liturgies are removed from everyday functions, if they see the Mass as something special, order and quiet will follow.

The Master of Ceremonies should also assist with the maintenance of order and quiet in the sacristy, even to the extent of asking concelebrants (who often have a lot of news to exchange and catching up to do) to keep the noise down in poorly sound-insulated sacristies. A period of prayer is recommended in the sacristy before and after Mass.

Chapter 10

BELLS AND SMELLS

Catholic Churches seldom have a ring of bells, one solitary Angelus bell is more normal.

It is good to retain the custom of ringing a bell for a period before Mass, as this not only encourages people not to be late, but also reminds an increasingly secular world that churches are still in use and have a loud and clear message to proclaim.

The Angelus can be rung at midday, although 6 am and 6 pm may be more difficult unless a recorded device is used. The Angelus is three separate rings of three strokes followed by a ring of nine strokes. In Eastertide and on Sundays outside Lent, the Regina Coeli can be rung: this is three rings of two strokes and one of six. At the consecration of the Mass a ring of three strokes may be rung at the elevation of the host and again at the elevation of the chalice.

The slow tolling of a bell at a funeral is a skilled task and the sacristan needs to have practised this.

A hand or sanctus bell is traditionally rung by the server at the consecration during Mass, and at the blessing during benediction. During the Easter Triduum bells are not used between the Gloria at the Mass of The Lord's Supper until the Gloria at the Easter Vigil. A wooden rattle or clapper can be used between times, although these days most places use nothing and maintain silence during the services of the triduum.

The use of incense is an ancient custom, used to hallow

or bless items or people. Incense is made from aromatic gums from various trees and shrubs or from the solidified oils from herbs and scented flowers. There is a great variety of scents available from church suppliers and from various abbeys and it is a good idea to vary the scent used in the different liturgical seasons. The grains of incense are sprinkled on charcoal disks which have been held to a flame in order to light them. In the sacristy it is sensible to have a small area where the charcoal and incense are stored and where the paraphanalia connected with incense is kept.

The vessel in which the charcoal and incense are burnt is called a thurible and the incense is kept in a boat and doled out using a spoon. The traditional thurible is supported by chains and needs a great deal of practice before it can be used proficiently. Where there is a shortage of servers, an open bowl on a stand in front of the altar can be used with plenty of lit charcoal in it on to which the priest or deacon sprinkles the incense at the appropriate time. The thurible is the hardest item in the sacristy to keep clean as, over a period of time, a layer of tar builds up inside it. This is best removed with a proprietary oven cleaner, taking all the precautions that the manufacturer recommends. Tongs are useful for holding the charcoal disk while lighting it.

An Incense Boat   The Incense Thurible
(with spoon for grains)

Chapter 11

THE CHURCH'S YEAR

Advent
There should be no flowers during Advent, but instead
an evergreen wreath large enough to be in scale with the
sanctuary, with three purple or violet and one pink candle.
A new candle is lit each Sunday as Advent advances, the
pink one being for the third Sunday when rose vestments
relieve the violet of the rest of Advent. The wreath should
be removed as the church is prepared for the Christmas
Vigil or midnight Mass.

Christmas
After the Fourth Sunday of Advent (not before!) the
church may be prepared for Christmas with trees, lights
and seasonal flowers such as poinsettias. The crib can be
set up somewhere in or outside the church, but not in the
sanctuary.

> If the manger is set up in the church, it must not be
> placed in the presbyterium. A place should be chosen
> that is suitable for prayer and devotion and is easily
> accessible by the faithful. (The Book of Blessings, 1554)

The crib need not be a sentimental rendition of the stable
scene, but can be a glorious representation of the paradise
promised by Christmas. The collection for the clergy needs
to be carefully labelled. All signs of Christmas should be
removed after the feast of the Baptism of Christ, the
Sunday after 6 January.

Epiphany (6 January or the following Sunday)

The three kings or magi should be placed in the crib.
Candlemas (2 February)

A procession with lit candles should precede the principal
Mass as detailed in *The Roman Missal* (page 530).

St Blaise (3 February)
Two candles blessed the previous day may be used to bless the throats of the faithful. (*Book of Blessings*, page 611)

Ash Wednesday and Lent
A preparation season for Easter begins with the imposition of ashes on Ash Wednesday. Ashes are the burnt palms of the previous year. If not purchased as ashes, the sacristan should burn and reduce the palms to a fine ash which should be placed in bowls to be blessed with holy water during the Mass (see *The Roman Missal*, page 74). The traditional colour for Lent is violet or purple with rose being used on the third Sunday as in Advent. Visual austerity is important during Lent. Flowers are not used, statues and crucifixes are covered in purple cloth for the period from Palm Sunday to the Easter Vigil. Stoops may be filled with sand or ashes for all of Lent, though there is no reference to this in the rubrics.

Passion (Palm) Sunday
Red is used for Passion (Palm) Sunday, the final Sunday of Lent when there should be a procession before the principle Mass (see *The Roman Missal*, page 122). Palm branches or other greenery should be carried. The uncovered processional cross should also be decorated with palm fronds. Holy water and a sprinkler are required at the start of the procession. Any attempt to include a donkey in this procession should be avoided as it will compromise the solemnity of the occasion. Stories of evacuated bowels and bladders and bitten children are too many to be ignored. For the reading of the passion, three lecterns with red falls should be prepared, one for each reader.

The Easter Triduum
This is the busiest time in the sacristan's year and demands a great deal of preparation. Holy Week manuals are available with detailed instructions in them for the sacristan and it is advisable for each parish to have one, but

there is room here to mention briefly the main preparations needed for the major services.

Holy (Maundy) Thursday
The altar of repose should be prepared during the afternoon of the day and is dressed in white fabric, with a few flowers and greenery to evoke the Garden of Gethsemane. Candles are placed on and around the altar. Where there is a solid floor, herbs and scented leaves can be strewn, but this is not advisable on carpet. The processional cross should be covered in white for today. The Mass of the Lord's Supper involves the *mandatum* (washing of feet) and the sacristan needs to have available, as well as everything for a solemn Mass, seats for those taking part, a jug of warm water and a large bowl, individual towels for each person, a *gremial* (apron) which can be an amice, a shoe horn, and a receptacle for the used towels. At the close of the rite a second jug of warm water and basin should be available for the celebrant with soap, brush and towel. For the procession to the altar of repose, the following are needed: incense, the humeral veil, an *umbrellino* (a large ceremonial umbrella usually covered with white or gold silk) or *canopy* (a large ceremonial cover, of white or gold silk, supported by four or six poles). It is appropriate for the congregation to carry lighted candles for the procession to the place of repose. On returning from the place of repose, the altars are stripped bare and everything movable should be removed from the sanctuary. At the close of 'watching', the Blessed Sacrament should be removed to a secure place (a safe), where there needs to be a corporal on which the ciborium is placed and a burning lamp nearby. Holy water stoops are emptied and cleaned.

Good Friday
If Tenebrae is celebrated on Good Friday and Holy Saturday mornings, the fifteen-branched candlestick should be placed on the sanctuary and the candles lit

before people arrive. The snuffer needs to be at hand for use during the saying of this office. In the afternoon liturgy the passion is read from three lecterns as on Palm Sunday. An altar cloth and corporal are placed on the credence table with the Roman Missal and a small bowl and finger towel. A crucifix (veiled if the first form of showing the cross is used) and two carrying candles are required at the place where the veneration of the cross begins. The veil should be either attached with tapes to the arms and upright of the cross or by velcro placed on the reverse. Two more candles and the humeral veil should be ready at the place of overnight reservation of the Eucharist. Crucifixes around the church are unveiled. Purificators or small towels should be available to wipe the cross between venerations The sacristan should carefully label the collection for the Holy Places.

Holy Saturday
The Easter vigil is the zenith of the sacristan's year. Many items are used this night that only appear once in the year. It is important that these items have been ordered, are clean and prepared, and are where they can be found easily. The sacristan needs to prepare a brazier with wood, coals and charcoal, or a container filled with salt soaked with surgical spirit, and have a flint lighter ready to light it a few minutes before the vigil starts. On a table nearby are placed a stylus (a dagger-type letter opener will do), the five brass incense grains, tongs, tapers, a shade for the paschal candle and most essentially a torch, and the sacramentary. It is wise to have a fire extinguisher at hand. The paschal candle should have been prepared with its transfer or design during the day, and candles for the people put with the service sheets at the gathering place. The empty thurible, boat with incense and the unlit acolytes' candles are carried in procession to the fire.

In the sanctuary, the altar should be prepared as for the major solemnity of the year and everything necessary for Mass prepared. This is the 'Mother of all Vigils' and merits all the best vestments, chalices and linens. The paschal candle stand should be prominently placed near the lectern for the singing of the Exsultet. The font should have been cleaned and filled and, if there is to be a baptism, everything requisite prepared. If water is to be blessed on the sanctuary and not at the font, a large vessel for carrying water to the font should be prominent. Holy water stoops are refilled after the Vigil. At the tabernacle, a lamp should be ready for lighting as the Blessed Sacrament is replaced in it after Holy Communion. The tabernacle key and the white veil also need to be available.

Easter Sunday
Everything for a major solemn liturgy needs to be prepared, again using the best vestments, chalices and linens. For the sprinkling during the renewal of baptismal promises, the Easter water blessed during the Vigil is used. If it is the custom to distribute eggs to the children, the sacristan must see that they are ordered and that there are baskets for them. The collection from the Vigil and all Easter Sunday Masses should be carefully labelled as the Easter gift to the clergy.

Pentecost
Many churches have vestments and altar frontals that depict the Holy Spirit; these should be used only for Pentecost, confirmations and votive Masses of the Holy Spirit. It is important that the sacristan uses the items at his or her disposal to best illustrate the seasons of the Church's year. By using the red pentecostal hangings on the feasts of martyrs, for instance, the issue becomes blurred and the importance of the seasons is not recognised.

The Easter season lasts until Pentecost and the church should be decorated in Easter colours: whites, yellows and greens for the entire season. For Pentecost, the colours should change dramatically to reds and golds to echo the flames of the Holy Spirit. The paschal candle is removed from the sanctuary to the baptistry at Pentecost. Between Easter Sunday and Pentecost, the candle should be lit for each Mass or service, but not during exposition and benediction.

Ordinary Time
The colour for this period in the year is green, but needs to be changed for all memorials, feasts and solemnities. Banners and posters reflecting the themes of the particular Sundays in Ordinary Time are available and can be used to good effect and are very useful catechetical aids. The church must not, however, become an art gallery with posters and banners left around once their relevance has ceased.

The Solemnity of the Body and Blood of Christ:
Thursday after Trinity Sunday (Corpus Christi)
If exposition follows on from the communion of the Mass, the sacristan must have everything needed for a Solemn Mass and exposition available on the sanctuary before Mass. The extra candles and throne are placed on the altar during the people's communion. If the period of exposition ends with a procession, the canopy or umbrellino, two thuribles, torches and candles for the people need to be prepared. As few visits to the sanctuary as possible should be made during exposition, but the sacristan must be on hand in case there is a rogue candle, or a lapse in the watching rota occurs. Any stational altars on the route of the procession need to be prepared with fabrics, candles and flowers and everything required for benediction should be available at the place where the procession ends.

Anniversary of Consecration
The twelve consecration lights around the walls of a church should be lit for Mass yearly on the anniversary of the consecration of a church and on the title feast of a church. They may also be lit on all solemnities.

Chapter 12

PRACTICAL LISTS

General Preparations

Before any service these basic preparations are necessary
> doors and exits unlocked
> lights on when necessary
> microphones set out and switched on
> hymn books available for congregation
> hymn numbers displayed
> pew sheets or missalettes available
> stoops filled
> votive candle stands filled with candles and emptied
>   of money

For the Celebration of Mass

On the altar
> at least one altar cloth
> two lit candles (may be carried in procession)
> *Book of Gospels* (if not carried in procession)
> microphone

Nearby
> a crucifix (may be carried in procession)
> a stand or ambo for the animator

At the celebrant's chair
> the Sacramentary on small lectern
> hymn book (if not carried)
> notices
> standing microphone (if used)

On the credence table
    set Missal on its stand
    layered chalice
    any extra chalices or ciboria
    extra purificators
    water cruet
    lavabo bowl and towel
    bell
    asperges vessel and sprinkler *(aspergillium)* if used

On the lectern or ambo
    Lectionary (may be carried in procession)
    microphone
    General Intercessions or Bidding Prayers

On the offertory table
    ciborium with hosts
    wine cruet
    empty collection bags

In the sacristy
    vestments for celebrant, concelebrants, deacons
    radio microphone
    hymn books for processionists (if carried)
    concelebration booklets

For a Solemn Mass

In addition to what is needed for a daily Mass, the following items will be required:
    two or four extra candles (on altar)
    thurible, charcoal, boat and incense (in sacristy)
    acolyte candles
    processional torches if used

For a Funeral Mass

In addition to what is needed for a daily Mass, the following items will be required:

the (funeral) pall
paschal candle and stand near to the coffin
Christian symbols, (crucifix and Bible) to place on the
    top of the coffin
holy water vessel and sprinkler
lit thurible and incense for use after communion

For Exposition and Benediction of the Blessed Sacrament

On the altar
drip cloth
corporal (unfolded)
the exposition throne
extra candles
the monstrance
the tabernacle key
any crucifix should be removed or screened

In the sanctuary
seats for celebrant and cantors

At the foot of the altar
cushion or prie dieu for celebrant
cushions for other ministers
the rites book
the bell
the humeral veil (nearby)

In the sacristy
cassock, cotta, stole and cope for celebrant
alb, stole and dalmatic for deacon (if attending)
thurible, charcoal, boat and incense
acolytes' candles or torches

For the Sacraments of the Church

Baptism: everything as for Mass with the addition of
a note of the child's names
a font of water

pouring vessel or shell
paschal candle
candle for the baptised
white garment (usually supplied by the family)
oils of chrism and baptism
cotton wool, bread and lemon
jug, basin and towel
the rites
the lectionary
booklets for parents and god-parents
the register needs to be available in the sacristy

Matrimony: everything as for Mass with the addition of
two prie dieu for the bride and groom
dish with the rings
holy water and sprinkler
the rites
hymn-sheet or booklet
the registers to be signed
a marriage candle

Reconciliation
rite of penance
crucifix and two lit candles on the altar (if a service)
   and at the place of individual confession
purple stole
the absolution
Bible
chair and/or a kneeler for the penitent
chair for the priest
act of contrition for the penitent

Confirmation: everything as for Mass with the addition of
the list of candidates
cards with confirmation names
the oil of chrism
cotton wool, bread and lemon

jug and bowl with warm water, soap and towel
Roman Pontifical (the bishop's secretary will usually
    bring this)

Ordination: everything as for a solemn Mass with the addition of
list of the candidates to be called
Roman Sacramentary
text of the litany of the saints
ordination cards

For a priestly ordination
a chasuble laid out in or near the sanctuary
the chalice and paten with the offertory gifts
the oil of chrism
cotton wool, bread and lemon
jug with warm water, bowl, soap and towel
ordination cards

For a diaconal ordination
a dalmatic and stole laid in or near the sanctuary
Book of the Gospels
the chalice and paten on the credence table

The other two sacraments have been adequately covered
elsewhere, the Anointing of the Sick in chapter 6, *The Sacred
Vessels and Holy Oils* and Holy Communion everywhere
that the Mass is mentioned.

ACKNOWLEDGEMENTS

The publishers wish to express their gratitude to the following for permission to include copyright material in this book:

Burns & Oates Ltd, Wellwood, North Farm Road, Tunbridge Wells, Kent, TN2 3QR for the extract from *Sacristan's Manual* by Father Dennis Murphy (Burns & Oates, 1950).

HarperCollins Publishers, 77-85 Fulham Palace Road, Hammersmith, London, W6 8JB for the short extract from *Code of Canon Law*, translated by the Canon Law Society of Great Britain & Ireland and published by HarperCollins Liturgical Publications.

International Committee on English in the Liturgy, Inc., 1522 K Street, NW, Suite 1000, Washington DC 20005-1202, USA for extracts from *The General Instruction on the Roman Missal* and the English translation of *The Roman Missal* © ICEL. All rights reserved. Used by permission.

The Liturgical Press, St John's Abbey, PO Box 7500, Collegeville, MN 56321-7500, USA for the extract from *Ceremonial of Bishops, revised by decree of the Second Vatican Ecumenical Council,* published by the Authority of Pope John Paul II in a translation printed by The Liturgical Press, 1989.

Every effort has been made to trace copyright owners of material and we hope that no copyright has been infringed. Pardon is sought and apology made if the contrary be the case, and a correction will be made in any reprint of this book.